PEEL BACK THE LAYERS

A book of Christian poetry

Marilyn Edwards

Kingdom
Publishers

Peel Back The Layers

A catalogue record for this book is available from the
British Library

ISBN: 978-1-913247-01-0

1st Edition by Kingdom Publishers
Kingdom Publishers
London, UK.

I would like firstly to thank the Holy Spirit for inspiration. Father God for equipping me with the ability to put pen to paper. My children, cousin and friend who listened to me going on about my writing.

CONTENTS

CHAPTER ONE   **SCRIPTURES EXEMPLIFIED**

Dry Bones	9
God Remnants	10
Gather the Crumbs	12
What a Price to Pay	13
Cain kills Abel	15
Lazarus	17

CHAPTER TWO   **LET IT GO**

Offence	19
Anger Controlled	21

CHAPTER THREE   **UNFOLD – TURN IT AROUND**

Street Life	22
Vision	23
Life Issues	24
Masked	25
Pursue, Overtake and Recover	27
Life Challenges	29
Deceiver	31
Tangled	33
Trust	34

CHAPTER FOUR   **MY HEART CRIES**

Flaws	36
Aching Heart it's Intense	38
Heart Cry	40
Secret Battles	42
Empty	44
Inner Self	46
It Hurts	48
Seasons	49
I Feel so Far Away	50
Don't Just Abandon Me	51
If I Should Fall	53

CHAPTER FIVE   **PRESSING THROUGH**

One, Two, Three	54
Pain !	55
Let Go	56
Just Pray	57
Reflection	58

Realty   60

Stand Tall   61

At a Standstill   63

Times   64

She Will Win   65

CHAPTER SIX   THE LORD AWAITS

What's Stopping you from Getting your Blessings   66

Jesus the Way   68

CHAPTER SEVEN   HERE I AM

Lord! Where are you?   69

Lord I've Come for a Chat   70

Here I am   72

To You O' Lord   74

Lord   76

Real   78

Why? Why? Why?   80

Knocking   82

Who am I   83

How Can I Ever Thank You   85

Shift   86

CHAPTER EIGHT   HUSH

Stillness   87

Be Still   88

Gentle Breeze   90

Calm   92

True Love   93

Hush   94

Refresh   96

Love Through the Holy Spirit   98

Peace   100

CHAPTER NINE   REFLECTION

Splendor   10

Love Song   10

Reflective   10

Structured   106

Imagine   10

CHAPTER TEN   MEMORIES

My Favourite Person   10

CHAPTER ONE
SCRIPTURES EXEMPLIFIED

—

Dry Bones

Dry bones, dry bones. Why?
Cause I've left my first love, God
And gone and try
To do things my way
And now I wonder
Why I have no relationship
With Jesus Christ who was crucified
Died for my sins
So that I could have eternal life.

Dry bones, my sins are many
Down in the valley with friends
Like me who refuse to surrender
And bow our knees.

Dry bones, dry bones
I need you no more
I come now to shut the door
Breathe upon me Lord
As I seek you for sure.

Dry bones, dry bones
I prophesy upon you, life
You shall live
As all to my Saviour I repent and give
My life, my being, everything
And unto the Father who created me I now cling.

—

God Remnants

Church cannot function on its own
God is the head and he sits on the throne
He needs a body like you and me
To spread His Word to a large degree.

If we do not come when we hear him call
How can His Word upon us fall?
And change our harden hearts from stone to flesh
Placing His Spirit in us and cleaning up our mess.

Alpha and Omega means the beginning and the end
So what God started He sure will end
He promise to build His Church and the gates of hell not prevail against it
He'll gather his sheep and remnants.

So if there are those who don't want to pray
He'll use his remnants to travail and lay
Lay at His alter with groans and tears
Crying out for souls so they will hear.

They never give up, they never sway
For they know they are called and their purpose is to stay
Grounded, steadfast and unmovable
So in God's eyes they will always be usable.

They'll stand through the test of time
And when the answer don't come
They won't sit and wine
They'll labor in prayer day and night
Calling on the God of Mercy to show them the light.

Remnants are a small part of what was large
But their value outweighs
For it speaks into the hearts of those who are hard
So as a Church, Father help us to stand
Looking onto you and not unto man.

Marilyn Edwards

Gather the Crumbs

Gather the crumbs, gather the crumbs
Bring it together to make one sum
The basket was empty and now it's full
Two fishes and five loaves.

Five thousand people did it feed
Some staring in disbelief
A miracle performed for that hour
Jesus showing his miracle working power.

Look at the time he turned water into wine
Making the last sweeter and more refine
Many did not realize what he had done
Even when all the wine was completely gone.

Even bigger miracles did He do
Cleansing the leper and healing them too.

What a Price to Pay

For the scriptures to be fulfilled
Judas had to betray the King
A kiss he used as a sign
To the chief priests and elders who were unkind.

He was judged by the Sanhedrin
Who found Him guilty!
And if that was not enough
They sought pleasure in slapping him.

As he went through this fate
The cock did crow
Peter denied him 3 times
Just as it had been foretold
Ashamed he felt when he realized he had sinned
Denying the Savior as his Redeeming King.

Peter watched as the chief priest took Jesus away
Later presenting him to Pilate bound in chains
He was questioned so that He could be accused
He spoke no word for what was the use.

It pleased the people to have him slain
And to have Barabbas the killer released
That was greater gain.

Pilate choose not to be a part of this wicked thing
But gave in to the people who screamed their penalty

Marilyn Edwards

Crucify him.
Pilate told all he washed his hands
Believing he was innocent of this devious plan.

The soldiers proceeded to take Jesus away
Stripping him of his own clothes
They dressed him in scarlet robe
A crown of thorns they placed on his head
And a reed in his right hand as the Bible says
They knelt and mocked him
Saying, hail King of the Jews
Your faith you cannot now refuse.

And if this was not all again they spat
Using the reed to beat his head
Blood dropped.

Mocking him they took off this robe
And placed back on him his own clothes.

As they led him away to be slain
With the final steps he took he was in pain
Golgotha was the place He was crucified
Beside two sinners but one received eternal life.

As soon as this was done Calvary cried out
The earth trembled, quaked and shout
When the Centurions recognise what they had done
They exclaimed truly this was God son.

For us he was born
And for us he died
To redeem man back to God's right side.

Cain kills Abel

You know I sat down one day
And I thought about Cain
Everyone talks of him as such a pain.
Yes he was jealous of his brother Abel
Because his offering to God was not approved
What he did not know in his heart is that God
Needed an offering he could use.
Not one that is strange or blemished he would have to refuse
But poor Cain did not understand that.

Think about it when he slew his brother
What was he going to prove?
That the keeper of the sheep was of no use
In his eyes he saw hate, jealousy which turned to rage
Should he have killed – NO
Even when he had committed such an act
God questioned him and he lied just like that.

Your brother's blood cries from the ground, shouts God
At first Cain could make no sound
But then answered God with his face caste down
My punishment is greater than I can bear
But I wonder if he said this with any flicker or tear.

Only thing we know is that his heart must have pounded with fear
For he was afraid of been slain
So what did God do!
Set a mark upon him so everyone would see
That if they touch him what their fate would be
The story of Cain just goes to show how good and evil
together cannot grow.

Lazarus

Lazarus was dead or so it seem
No movement just stillness was seen
No light that shone but darkness unknown
That's how dead Lazarus was.

Tomb and enclosed, presumed dead by most
A darkness that was endless, bleak, black and friendless.
Lazarus did not know his faith
Graveyard dead he would not wake.
Dead clothes he wore, the colour a bore
Yes! Lazarus was dead.

His death was reported to the source of life
Jesus the only living Christ
Tears fell, sorrow felt
Yes! Lazarus was dead.

What was the purpose of his death?
To show Jesus Christ and his righteousness
Yes! And to bring glory to His name
And show the world dead things can come back
To life again.
At the tomb, he Lazarus was called

Come forth and stand tall
A command for the dead clothes to fall
Loose him and let him go
He's not dead at all.

CHAPTER TWO
LET IT GO

—

Offence

Offence! Oh no, what have I done
I've gone and used my unruly tongue
To speak and utter words that is so mean
"Don't look at me like that", I say
When piercing eyes return a gaze
Looking at me with venom and hate.

I won't take it back I think to myself
She deserved it well.
Am I unkind in my heart, I question
A little voice respond and say,
"No corrupt communication".

The tongue, the tongue, how great a matter
A fire it can kindle
It can defile
Be so unkind
That's the reason many pay it so much mind.

It's an unruly evil, full of deadly poison
I hear a shout
Tame it, tame it
You can if you pull down the strongholds using the word of God.

Renew your mind and your heart will follow
Do it today, don't leave it to tomorrow
God's word is sure and it must stand
Don't use your tongue to hurt or offend another man.
And if you do or someone offends you
Forgive and repent
Be quick to stop it, block it and put a dot at the end of it
So that words coming forth edifies, builds up and not tear down
You can do it
Just put a smile on your face and not a frown.

Anger Controlled

Anger! Be angry and sin not says God
Anger can make your countenance sad
It can be ugly when not stopped in its track.

Anger is displayed in many ways
Rage, hate, big distaste
It can grip all of sudden
When tempers flaws, then anger glares
But how do the word sin appear.

Well Jesus took it when he was slain
So we his children don't have to try to stop it in vain
Don't get me wrong
It can be hard to do
Because this emotion can be terrible when it hits you.

Some can control it
Some find it hard
But the Word of God remember is our rear guard
We can crush it, break it, we can use the hammer
The Word of God to deflate it.

CHAPTER THREE
TURN IT AROUND

—

Street Life

There are people on the street
With nowhere to sleep and nothing to eat
But I know Lord you are able
To stop their daily weep.

You are able to bring them through
To a world that looks new
You are able to show the way
The way to fill their every day.

With goodness and mercy Lord
You can take the weak and make them strong
Confound the mighty and make the weak man someone.

So Lord I bless and I praise you
For your love, your peace, my Lord
That surpasses all understanding.

You said, my peace I leave with you
And now I ask you to pour your peace
Upon your people.

——

Vision

When I went into the shops today
I was surprised but not dismayed
An idea came into my head
You can do just like they have
Remember God says run
Write the vision it will not tarry.

How do I do this I ask?
It seems to be too hard a task
Then I heard
Risk it like most have done
They did not hang on or wait around.

God gives purpose to every man
A vision in all men plans
It's then up to man to see it through
All God can do is provide the vision to you.

My mind was transfixed
OK! I said that's it
No more fear because this does not fit
You have told me to fear no man
Come on, look how the children of Israel
Crossed the red sea unto dry land.

Run, run with it. You can and you will do it.

Marilyn Edwards

Life Issues

Have you ever had a situation that's gotten you down?
Your face is caste to the ground
You try to stand but you are about to fall
You look up and down to try and stand tall.

Faith resides on the inside but oh no, it's weaken and cannot grow
Situations are too much to bear
Here comes a drop, here comes a tear.

You thought you had conquered but the hurt and pain has won
You break down and fall with a bang
Strong people don't become weak
That's what you thought before you went to sleep.

But waking up the pain and hurt is intense
What you are holding is offense
You scream, hallow and bawl
Frightened because all is gone.

No money, no friends, children taken where does it end
No defense! Husband ran off with a friend
Debts to pay, feeling dazed
It's OK, Jesus Christ will show the way.

Masked

Masked that's what I've been wearing
There's no point contemplating
For the expressions does not fit the heart
They are measures and inches apart.

Masked over, features not telling
Everything within swelling
What would it be like to take off the mask?
Come naked, starring at each heart.

Ones that speaks truth and no lie
The ones that would not criticize
And tear with their tongues
But put a smile on to turn it upside down
Forgetting that their own heart can also unfold
The mask they wear can also become known.

Mask come off, Jesus is the health of my countenance
He'll make my mountain to stand strong
He never leave nor forsake me but will walk with me along
He'll pick me up and turn me around
And plant my feet on solid ground.

Masked, that's just talk, take it off
Look at your face in the glass (WORD)
And shine like you've been told
For the Word of God is like pure gold
No more mask!

Pursue, Overtake and Recover

Plans many times are mans
Egocentric he must have meant it
No one can tell him what to do
Plans sometimes plenty, sometimes few.

God's plans he has for each man
For direction, no complications
Yes sometimes struggles, sometimes muddles
But in the end it does not work out wrong.

Plan, pursue and structure
Everything in life must be in order
For Jesus says, *"I know the plans I have for you*
Plans for welfare not calamity in everything you do
I will lead you in a way you know not
Yes that's a fact
Nothing, but you cannot stop that".

The Word sometimes we don't want to follow
A lamp to our path to lead us tomorrow
Sharp able to cut like a sword
Brake barriers that wants to close some doors.

Lord I come to ask you a question

Marilyn Edwards

You spoke to me some time back
Stating things you want me to do
And that there'll be no lack.

You said, you hear me and my answer is here
"What do you mean by that?"
Maybe I ought to know but right now I feel flat.

◼◼

Life Challenges

The pain that is felt inside
Only self can hide
Hidden in the depth of ones' being
It cannot be seen.

Anger burst, filthy words
Spilling from a heart that hurts
Hiding true feelings even though it needs healing.

Frightened that you will be judged
But many are there
Many do fear
If only they could just disappear.

It's not like it wants to go away
Bathing with drinks and hard cocaine
Hoping it would numb the pain.

It's frightening all the abuse
Filthy hands swinging through
Sadden eyes looks from where it would strike
Wondering if there is anywhere to hide.

Marilyn Edwards

In the end it did numb
That thing you take instead of a gun
It would be the easiest thing to do
But a cry inside says no not you
A bigger plan is about to unfold
Only hold on it will be told.

Deceiver

Am I being deceived when I do wrong?
Is it the devil holding my hand?
Is my stronghold being let down?
Am I no longer a part of the crown?
The crown of glory that takes me to heaven
Or am I just a football for the devil.

What do I do at these times?
Suffer my guilt or ask God's advice
And then turn around and kick the devil twice?

Am I so low in blessings that I can fall?
Should not my blessings be rich and tall?
Why then do I question my worth?
Is it the devil making me feel like dirt?

Tell me Father Yahweh what to do
I am your child and I call on you
Now that I have fallen I need to know
Are my guardian angels around to show?
To show me you the Rock, your solid ground
So that I may place my feet down without a frown

And for you to build me back up and turn me right around
So that my spirit can glorify the Crown.

So I say to everyone
Do not be deceived
It is the devils way of stealing your creed.

Tangled

Tangled in sin
Who said you would win
It's hard to see what it could have been
Old situations now coming clean.

Marilyn Edwards

Trust

Do you know Jesus?
Do you truly know him?
Is he part of everything you do?
Would you say he supplies all your needs?
Is he your source and your strength indeed?

Is he the first person you talk to each waking day?
Is he the last person to whom you kneel down and pray?
Or are you just one of them who don't really believe
Is your heart far from what you speak?

Is he the closet friend you have?
Is he the one you lean on when sad?
Through test and trials
Is he the Rock in which you hide?

Ask yourself this question, PLEASE!
How much do you know him?
And is it a knowing that you can keep
When the storms comes are you blown
Or do you always stand firm.

Do you trust he makes every crocked path straight?
And is always there when you wake
Do you believe His yoke is easy and his burden light?
Or is this mistake.

Are you connected to the living Vine?
Grafted in him and not to the world that can be so unkind
Do you look to Him the hills from whence your help comes?
The Creator of heaven and earth
Or are you running back and forth.
He says, trust in me with all your heart
Lean not on your own understanding and I will direct your path.

He tells us in him we live and move and have our being
He created us in his image and when he did it he was pleased
Whey then do you always let him pass by
When he is knocking and saying for you I died.

Do you believe he can forgive your sins?
Cleanse you from all unrighteousness within
Remember it's your heart He seeks
Whilst man looks at the outside first to see if it please.

Don't shy away from His call
Once forgiven your sins like scarlet He will not recall.

CHAPTER FOUR
MY HEART CRIES

—

Flaws

Lord, I know that I have been all over the place and not very keen
Many things have taken over and I never seem to glean
I feel like a ton of brick has been placed upon me
Heaviness in totality
Others don't see what they do
Maybe myself too.

Why is it I am so thick meshed in my head?
I just said, crying tears so many times
Heart cannot unwind
Plumbing, plumbing I'm tired of jumping
Having many things to say
I forgive, I forgive
Help me Lord to continually pray.

Tears right now wants to come
I really wish I could talk openly to someone
It's a lonely place to be
Thinking others are holier than me.

Be real with yourself I say, for God will show the way
He has done I am sure

But I hide
Is it me or is it pride.

Forgive me Lord
For I know I am wrong when I go against your plan
Let your will be done not mine
Help me lord to just let go and unwind
And let thine will be done in this time.

Marilyn Edwards

Aching Heart it's Intense

If hearts could not wound my one would
If pain could speak my one should
If tears could not flow mine would still drop
If life could say what would happen at every stop.

The pain, the hurt, the wants, the need
It continues and continues to repeat
Emotions boiling still it's too hot
People taking every last drop.

We've become so heartless
It's a joke
No one any longer want to hold
To care, to hug, to love but just to take
And it does not matter whether it aches.

We are all looking for love, care, someone near
But it's hard because no one wants to share
Selfishness prevails and drops
Harden hearts going Blop! Blop!

When emotionless eyes can look at you
And say I've done nothing wrong
It's you I'm ok

And the heart and mind know it's not true
But because of habit truth refuse.

Lord I made myself come to this place
Yet it's like I cannot wake, and shake
And say, look no way this is a big, big mistake
Leave it, don't cleave to it
There's too much fake, out to draw pull and make
Jesus you told us to walk your way
Yet in our human flesh we continually sway.

Look beyond the false smile
Actions that make you feel ok for a while
Then not long after it repeats itself
And you're back at that place again.

If the truth be said, it stinks and it's dread
But no don't climb into bed
Stand up, take stock, block it, and duck it
Mind blowing though it may seem
There's no need to scream.

It knows no better
Its place is fun
Feelings are not important
You may as well see it like using a gun.

Shoot at the target
And close your eyes
When you open it there's no surprise
It did not hurt you but someone else
So what does it matter, well!

Heart Cry

I feel sick and so numb
I feel all alone
Like I'm on my own
Emptiness shut up inside
Wanting, seeking ever cleaving
To possibly what's not mine.

Scared to shift
Feels too swift
But if I could be strong
And say to myself that's wrong thinking
Stop the blinking, hinkling and do something.

When was the last time I truly smiled?
Emptied my true feelings from inside
Felt no way to let things out
Even if muddled, I still need to shout.

Loneliness! it's not nice
Many of us don't admit it because of pride
What is there to hide?

I need an embrace
I need it in haste
Lord help me for it really aches
Love where does it hide
When there are deep feelings inside.

Marilyn Edwards

Secret Battles

I could not sleep
Lots of things going through my head
It felt dread
Negative thoughts, confusion starts
Too many questions answered far apart.

Noise! My mind confused
I hate it, I hate it! How can I refuse?
The thoughts won't go
I don't want them to show
To surface and flow
Secret battles, Oh God I know.

Like a mountain that is high
I feel I need to jump, punch
Run or get a gun, shout stop
Block make it stop, secret battles.

Where? Where is everyone?
I thought we all were one
Who says, was it just I
No peace, peace, I began to cry.

I twist and turned on my bed
My head, my head, make it stop
The thoughts, the thoughts
How long they last, secret battles
Oh God they are too much hassle.

I tried to clear the thoughts I had
But more was added, a cry, a tear
Even big time fear
Secret battles, who out there cares.

Marilyn Edwards

Empty

Lord help me to persevere
I feel naked, I feel bare
Stripped of all I thought I had
Taken back with one grab.

Help me to never say, oh no! What?
Questions that show that I have come a long way
Never to wean or complain
Emptied by the aches and pain.
Heart filled, thoughts up
Thinking the right things, becoming tough.

I feel the tears wanting to flow
Eyes filling up with water it stores
But it won't come
It's not going to drop, too many issues
If I started it would not stop.

Overwhelmed, maybe, I am not sure
Need you to hold me close and secure
Yeah many times I don't understand
What is happening in my mortal man?

I hold my head up, hands on chin
Thinking, blinking yes the light looks dim
Help me to understand dear Lord
Bring revelation to this broken heart.

I look to the left and I look to the right
Sorrow filled on both my sides
Will I ever understand how it goes?
Support it must be close.

Inner Self

My self-dignity
It screams at me
It says: "How can you be so naive?"
It tells me off all the time
And makes me take time to unwind
Place my thoughts on the side
And looking at what else besides.

In the emptiest moments I quail
Because many things I do is so pale
I'm actually ashamed to say
Within my heart I continually sway
Lord do I know myself
And am I listening to you
As in my mind things melt
And my outer shell wants to swell.

Tiredness all the time as many things trouble my mind
I try to take them out of my head
Focusing on the Word of God instead
But did you know your mind can become so transfixed
With issues that cause you not to shine

Imaginations that you try to throw
But each time it just does not want to go.

You use the Word continually to caste down vanity
Things that will not benefit you in any degree
The blood of Jesus Christ cries from your lips
Suddenly, that heavy brick leaves you like a lick
Quick, quick, quick.

Marilyn Edwards

It Hurts

If hearts could speak of brokenness
Mine would surely pass the test
If minds could be seen
Mine would not be too keen
For all to see the confusion that is set.

If eyes could follow each thoughts that persist
I can tell you mine would surely resist
If ears could hear those secret thoughts
Mine! Yes, would not be first at the start.

What memories I have of all that's gone by
Like a flicker in the sky
Good ones, bad ones, sometimes ugly
Hopes and expectations dashed
Smashed, why? Why? On my!

Seasons

Have you ever just poured the tears that would not stop?
Rolled up into a ball and cried until you feel you would pop
Because the ache and pain is too much to bear
Crying with your heart and feeling like it would tear.

Have you ever just starred and remained transfixed
Not knowing when the clock ticked
Dazed from your situation
Not knowing when it will end
Waiting, praying and saying
Have you?

Marilyn Edwards

I Feel so Far Away

Lord, why do I feel so far from you
Been fed so much food
But yet I feel empty and confused.

Why lord! Why?
Am I not at the place I should be?
Drinking milk not digesting solid meat
It's like something is missing
Taken away yet I ask
What could it be?

That's why sometimes I don't take breaks
Cause it always seems to sway
The focus and the discipline –
No, no, the enemy cannot win

Tiredness seems to control
But I bind it down and remain bold
Distractions coming from all parts
Specially that within the heart

Lord I don't want to feel you are far
Cause I need you in this war
Cause you promise to subdue the enemy under my feet
Thank you lord this promise you will keep.

Don't Just Abandon Me

Daddy, when I was conceived
You were there with me
As your seed connected with my mother's egg
You may not have known conception took place
But you were there nevertheless.

As I grew within the walls of my mothers' womb
You may still not have noticed
But my mother did.

When she saw her growing tummy
And her enlarged breast
You may also have seen it
Then again, maybe not.

As I developed within the walls
Protected from the world outside
Comfortable with the world within
Did you hold mummy hand?
And stand up by her side as a man.

When I was born did joy fill your heart?
Or were you worlds apart

Did you hear my first cry?
Or see my first smile.

As I grew and my features changed
And I cried for you
Did you hear or were you too far away
Daddy, did you even care
Daddy, the question is
Why! Did you abandon me?

I'm told when my father or mother forsake me
Then the Lord will take me up
These words became a comfort
After many years of tears
Unanswered questions that bugged me down
Now all the answers appeared.

My Saviour suffered more than I
And yet he was prepared to die
Thank you Jesus
That you did not abandon me.

If I Should Fall

If I should fall
Shall I rise more powerful?
Or do I stay crouched down
Am I not just flesh and bone?
No stronger than a lion
Who is seen as a strongest beast.

Are the fishes of the sea not smaller than me?
Yet when they swim to the bottom of the sea
Do they not rise above that level?
So why should I continue to crouch down
When the only thing this will do is help me to fall.

CHAPTER FIVE
PRESSING THROUGH

One, Two, Three

Looking around, what can I see?
Many, many issues staring at me
Too many to count 1, 2, 3
Challenges, challenges to large degree
When will it end?
When will it stop?
Could this be the last drop?

How can so many things come at once?
Life like a roller coaster with lots of things
Running up, running down, like a stream
It goes round and round never coming down.

Lord help me to stand strong
The race is not for the swift
But it is for those who endure to the end
For this reason Jesus Christ was sent.

Pain !

Pain! I thought I knew pain
But not like this
When people become selfish
They cause you pain but don't see
They think they do you no wrong
But when you're on the other end
Pain can make you bend.

Pain! Such pain and hurt felt inside
You feel let down used and casted aside
How can another man be so heartless?
As long as they are able to do what they want
It don't matter whether it hurts another
I never thought I would get this from a brother.

Hurts and aches they become so use to inflicting
It then becomes no shame, care or fear
If brokenness could describe what I feel inside
It would not come near to what I hide
Only when you go through it you will understand
Help me lord to stop focusing on man.

Marilyn Edwards

Let Go

I never thought I would get to a place
Where I feel lonely like I'm in space
Loneliness seems to want to take control
But behind I say to you who is trying to come forth bold
Not my portion, not my friend
I caste you down into that pen
Let go, I don't want you
I have friendships and not just a few.

If you have ever felt lonely, it's not at all nice
It puts itself forward and sometimes it can make you feel tight
Empty, overwhelmed with self-pity
Especially when you call upon someone and they are busy.

Just Pray

I lean my head upon my hands and wonder why this way
Holding up myself less I begin to sway.
Curling up into a ball
Wishing I could bounce out of it all.
Issues, needing tissues to wipe it away
Why don't I just pray?

Marilyn Edwards

Reflection

Right now I sit on my bed
Many things going on in my head
Trying to focus on what comes next
Trying not to do things whilst I'm vex.

I sit and wonder what could have been
Even if I had been keen
Truly I wonder what I've missed
Cause it feels like I've experience a ton of bricks.

You see people and you think you know
You look for changes things that show
But many of us have stinking thinking
Self, self, that's what's real
Nobody wants to any longer share even a meal.

Self, self, that's what cries out
Even if it hurts
Does not matter it's self that counts.

Jesus became selfless
Thought of others

Until he emptied all
All of himself so he could give
What he knew man would need to live.

I totally surrender all to you Lord
Hurts, pains, let downs and frustrations
I was not missing anything
Because what I see is self and stinking, thinking.

Marilyn Edwards

Reality

I feel like everything has been taken
I feel so empty inside
I sit in my little corner
Holding my hands by my side.

I question many things praying it is not so
But I must look at reality
Because in front of me it glows.
I look deep within saying
Don't be confused
Make a plan stick to it
Ticking off one by one.

I'm hurting, filled with disappointments
But God says He will work it out
What is meant for bad to good.

God is not a God of confusion
He says, His plans for us, are for welfare and not calamity
Perfecting everything in his hands
Peace, Gods' peace stands
Let not my heart be troubled
Cause it will if I let man.

Stand Tall

Right now my heart aches
Feels like it's going to brake
Wanting tears to fall
But no way, I'm going to stand tall.

Memories of many things
Hopes and dreams seems so glim
When at one time everything was so right
Now it seems like only a flicker of light.

Why do I hurt so easily?
Wanting always to cry to ease it
Trying so hard to be strong
Even when it's not me that's wrong.

Is it so much to ask for Lord
The things you promised
I thought I was walking true
At the time it seemed that everything
Was waiting for me in a queue.

Marilyn Edwards

Sadden by little revelation
Eyes closed, not seeing things clear
Keep wanting just to stare
Shaking my head in disbelief
Wanting to feel that total relief.

Is it so hard to want to say, I need
Tell me is it so hard for one to please
What is it we are looking for?
Walking far apart
Not meeting truly in our hearts.

At a Standstill

At a standstill
Where is the hill
I slowly have to climb
Blame myself
Yes I do, all the mistake is mine.

Still my heart yearns for such things
I know I desire to find
Why so hard Lord
Which card do I now bring from behind?

I sit and wonder why so high a climb
Some hills are high, some hills are low
Why the high one for me.

My heart can't explain the ache
It's so deep within
My face will show you only
What I want you to think.

Marilyn Edwards

Times

There has been times in my life when I felt alone
Times when I felt on my own
Times in my life when I felt I had no friends
Times when I felt I could not go on
Times when everything I did felt wrong
But one thing I know now
It was God's way of making me strong
For the road I need to follow each day as I go along.

So the time came when I recognized that
The only love I could depend on
For the rest of my life
Was that of the Saviour, Jesus Christ
Who is understanding and kind
And will never leave me nor the rest of mankind.

So if you feel the things I've just described
You have not yet found the love of God and Jesus Christ.

She Will Win

I saw my daughter cry today
Tears poured down
Into the tissues goes issues
Aching heart
Words far apart
Not knowing why she feels this way
Words she utters but heart cannot say.

Confusion, illusions, I bind you down in Jesus name
You cannot have your way
Jesus bled and died to make everything alright
She will win, she will win
She is a conqueror Lord help her understand this within
A hug making things around her seem real
When deep down she needs to recognise and be healed.

CHAPTER SIX
THE LORD AWAITS

—

What's Stopping you from Getting your Blessings

Blessings are gifts from God
Not something we've always had
Don't get me wrong it's always been there
Because God promised them to us
If we would hearken and hear.
So what's stopping us from getting them?
Let's just think awhile!

Do we really believe Jesus Christ was crucified?
And was resurrected for all mankind
Do we believe Jesus Christ is the son of God?
The expressed image of His person.

Do we believe the Word we read?
Is Jesus Christ himself indeed
Are we satisfied in Him we can do all things?
And that we are overcomers
Always able to win.

Do we believe He is Gods' Son?
Who was and is and is to come

Do we believe He is holy and most divine?
Who came to rescue all of mankind?

Do we believe he died and rose again?
Believe and live the word he says
Is there somewhere in our being
Where we pray, praise and worship
Do we believe that God hears us and will reply?

If we say we do, then why are some still confused
Find it hard to express a love he gave us, so we can be bless
His love is deep, it is wide
Cannot be measured, nor caste aside
Unless that's what you want to do
He is real, He is there for you.

Just seek and you shall find
Knock and the door shall be open
Ask you shall receive
These are His promises that He will keep.

Jesus the Way

What does it profit a man to gain the world and lose his soul?
To run after treasures untold
To entangle oneself in only the world way
And disregard heavens domain.

The light of day only shines once
The lifetime of that person stands
But once the light of day has gone
The soul within must stand alone
And see what his future holds.

The road is wide, where Satan hides, on the inside
The road to heaven, oh you guess, its way is narrow.
Our gain is therefore not on earth
Where man tries to get everything he can
Regardless of how devious his plans.

If in this life there was no hope
Do you suppose anyone would strive?
To perfect that which only God can do
And leave it to him to fulfill it too.

CHAPTER SEVEN
HERE I AM

—

Lord! Where are you?

Lord, where are you when I call
I feel empty I feel small
Like I am against a wall
Knocking, banging and shouting
I cannot feel the warmth
Praise and prayer a struggle
Lord take me out of this muddle.

Feeling tired cannot get out of bed
When I do get up my head feels empty
BUT other things around me is plenty.

Dress me, protect me and cover me
Armor me with your weapon
Take me to the throne room of grace
And deliver me from the enemy in haste
The Blood, the Blood
Strengthen me with your love.

I confess out of the pit I step
No longer want to keep this mess
A mind of Christ is what I posses
Jesus Christ and righteousness.

Lord I've Come for a Chat

Lord how are you today? Just calling to say, "Hi"
At first I was going to question and ask you why
But then I remembered you know my heart and hear my cry
So I have decided no, I'll come for a chat instead.

You made the world Lord, and the seasons therein
The birds, the bees, the plants, the trees and everything within
When I look at what I see
Yes, Lord it amazes me, how you speak and we cannot see
It truly amazes me.

At times when I've walked down the road
And looked up at the sky
Seeing the beauty of the firmament
All I could do was sigh
Because you see that again is how you speak.

Then my eyes look down at the ground
And I'm reminded of the endless depth
How can we, your chosen ones really truly forget?
It amazes me.

No depth, no width, no height but only deep
Lord again I see how you speak.

Then you show me the Word and I am truly amazed
How man could say it came from another
And not through your inspired power
Again, it amazes me.

Marilyn Edwards

Here I am

Dear Lord, I missed you so much
Your gentle and tender touch
You who hold me every day
For months you seemed so far away.

I closely longed to feel your arms
Where I can and always feel warm
I considered hard and long
But then I realized that when I feel weak
That's when you make me strong.

I prayed and cried unto you
A heart that was heavy and confused
Many times I felt I could not penetrate
The door that would allow me to escape.

It felt like the rain had come
But then when it had stopped came the storm
I struggled to hold on
Slipping and sliding along.

The Word would come then it would go
A song or two would also show

Though my voice said the word
My heart could not comprehend the verb.

In tenseness and anxiety
I remembered the Word has no profit unless believed
My heart cried out what my mouth could not conceive.

I love you Jesus so very much
The tears cannot express enough
You've been so tender and so kind
You did not leave me at any time.

I thank you for destroying my Goliath
And saving me from the lion's den
For taking me across the stormy sea
And through the wilderness where I learnt patience
Longsuffering and faith in much degree.

Thank you Jesus that you did not give me over as a bait
The snare is broken and I'm escaped.

Marilyn Edwards

To You O'Lord

To you O' Lord, I give my all
In you O' Lord, is everything
My life, my being, salvation O' King.

When I look back and see
The path you took me from
A bleak dark place
I thought was bright
Now I realize there was only a dim light

It's all a lie the truth not told
A looking glass that can unfold
To reveal the truth that's hidden
It seems now that all was
And some are still in prison.

The chains that bind
The cuffs that hold
The world just a great big black hole
No doorway that one can go through
Just surrounded by walls with no view.

Sometimes I look and what I see is false
It's not real, it's a lie, surrounded by an appetite
One that brings death and pain
Even though most understand it to be gain.

I cannot believe that's where I was
In this game of great pretence
Bound in chains
Fill with the world deceit
Running to and fro to make ends meet.

Following a concept that has been passed down
A world with religious belief that only bounds
Believing that man in his feebleness is complete.

How often do we go and tell
Wide is the road that leads to hell
And many enter therein
Narrow is the road that leads to life
And only a few shall enter.

Lord

Lord, you are Holy
Lord, you are my Deliver
You took me from the dust
And made me to praise you.

So I say to you
Thank you for what you do
You gave me grace with haste
You gave me pride to stand and not hide
You said in your Word
Seek me and you shall find
That was not just for me
But all of mankind.

So I say again
You are my only friend
Through thick and thin
I know I will win
For you are my strength
My fortress too
My deliverance comes from you.

So I reverence your name
That will always be the same
I give you praise
I exalt you oh Lord
For you Lord are my saving Grace,
MY ALL, yes Lord.

Marilyn Edwards

Real

One day I questioned who I was
A voice came into my head
Asking me if I heard what I just said
I looked around
But there was no one to be found
I felt a little frighten as I felt my heart pound
Then I heard the voice again saying,
"Do not be afraid
It is I the Lord guiding your way".

I felt a sudden calm
Like just after a storm
My heart began to feel very, very warm
Then a prayer came to me
And this is what it said:

"The Lord is your founder
Might and your strength
He will always love you
No matter what your creed
He is forgiving and open to all your needs.

He is the Saviour of all mankind
Blessed is the man who will live his life in me
He will reap all heavenly blessings you see
Because he will be faithful through and through
And if he fails me
This is what he must do
Repent and ask for forgiveness but it needs to be true."

Why? Why? Why?

Lord why do I sit down so many times and cry
Sadness taking over what should be joy
Expectations such a ploy
Secret motives, what else can it be
Every moment staring at me.

What are words when actions do not prevail?
Emptiness just like an open vale
Am I so sensitive I cannot see above?
My thoughts so intense, deep!
In heaps so much so that at times I feel to weep.

But at such times you give me strength
To rise back up and call on you my friend
But there are times when I hold everything inside
Yes! Cause I know if I should speak what I would hear
Moments and memories soon disappear.

How can I simply see what could have and should be
Waking moments remembering in large degree
I cannot understand sometimes
Why I keep so many things on my mind.

I hurt and yet still I cling
Why! Why! Why I sing
Help me Lord to see clear
I no longer want to weep or cry a tear.

Marilyn Edwards

Knocking

Lord here I am again
Sometimes I shy away from you
You are the only one who truly knows what we go through
I'm sorry that sometimes I may try to hide
But in all the things I've done
I pray you're still at my side.

Who am I

Why should I hide myself away?
Sin through Jesus Christ was slain
Taken and placed on the cross
So that none of us could be lost.

Why then is it so hard to do
The right thing and not to be confused
With the many issues of life
That comes into our sight.

Why should my heart go dim?
When to Jesus I can cling
Every day I ask the question
Who am I within?

The light when turned on is bright
Even for those with no sight
But darkness in the world sometimes
Tries to hide it behind
But it cannot work that way you see
Because darkness is comprehended by the light so let it be.

Why do the tears come in between?
Secret motives seems more keen
Understanding our dreams
Others clouding it in between
Clarity, familiarity, truth and equality.

How Can I Ever Thank You

Lord how can I ever thank you enough?
For all you have done for me
You wipe away the tears I weep
You take me off my knees to my feet
You give me a keeping peace
How can I ever thank you enough.

Sometimes in my heart I feel fear
But I know lord you are always near?
In my mind I hear not what I want to
Then I remember certain words I can refuse
Because you have given me love, power and a sound mind
So I can throw down every word that is unkind.

It's funny you know lord
That even when we profess
Words can still destroy us when we go through a test
Our minds go blank
Can sometimes blow up like a tank
The Words of life can become few
But I realize as long I say Jesus Christ I am loosed.

Shift

Incline my ears to hear you Lord
To hear what you want to say
Anoint my lips of clay.

Incline my heart to seek you Lord
So you can lead my way
My mind, my soul, my goal is never to sway.

Incline my will to your will Lord
So that I'll follow your path
Doing what you want me to
Truly from my heart.

Entwine my spirit with yours Lord
As you keep me by your side
Let my foot remain steadfast
So that I do not slip or slide.

CHAPTER EIGHT
HUSH

Stillness

It's quiet but I can still hear riot
Listen and be still!
Trees blowing, overflowing
Over and above everything.

Breeze, ease, starting to sneeze
The wind rife against the atmosphere
Cleverly blowing down all cares
Heading towards the grimmest place
Not even doing it in haste.

Marilyn Edwards

Be Still

Sometimes I feel all alone
I feel like I'm on my own
Trying to hear that still small voice
Speaking words of wisdom.

When I call to check things out
Many times I feel maybe I should shout
But then I remember be still.

You tell me, Lord
"Be still and know that I am God
Because you don't hear me doesn't mean I'm gone
My voice can be very still and calm
Daughter be perfectly still.

Rest in me, I never fail
Rest in me you will prevail
Rest in me for when you are weak I am strong
Rest in me and I will carry you along."

Am I wrong Lord to ask you, why?
I cannot hear you when I cry
Everything seems very, very rough

Bring me through Lord, bring me through.

In my waiting I seek your patience
In my waiting I seek your joy
In my waiting I seek your love
Help me Jesus from above.

Jehovah Jireh, my provider
Jehovah Nissi, the Lord my banner
Jehovah Rapha, the Lord my healer
Elohim, Eternal Creator.

Gentle Breeze

Gentle, gentle as a breeze
So I must be with much ease
As the Holy Spirit is like a dove
Help me Lord to embrace your love.

People see me they see pale
They don't understand the gale
The things that life has thrown but I still prevail.

They see what I want them to see
They will know by a small degree
Heart, mind and soul they cannot perceive.

The things I believe in
That I held onto
Seem to have gone astray
Memories fade on what I use to do and say.

The things I wanted and thought I had
At least it seems like it was not that bad
Sad, but not mad
Who can I talk to, to make it, not break it.

Words I hear that's contrary
Words that does not flow
Hearts that do not understand
That we are not just mere man
God's plan it must stand
On His Word we must land.

Marilyn Edwards

Calm

The billows blow, the wind bluster below
The waves it raises high then low
It rustles rough, then it slows
Sometimes its height is like a mountain
Then it appears like the valley
Bustles, hustles, as it hits against the rocks and stones
Fiercely raging never mistaking where it plans to go.

I cry calm, yes you storm
Receive the Word that formed you
Before the foundation was born
You must be still, quiet so I can feel tranquil
A place where I can find safety and calm
No more bustles, no more fuss
But peace as I find safety in God's arm.

True Love

No ounce of love can I give
But that to which I truly lived
Shared with me in full not in part
Straight from the heart.

How can I know how it feels
To love unconditionally
When for me it has not been real
Oh! But how my heavenly Father gives
Unconditional love to its fullest.

I learn to understand His love
Endless sent from above
Sinless, selfless it comes upon me like a dove.

We portion love, we give it in measures
Depending on who we treasure
But Christ love is full and sure
Loving everyone rich or poor.

Marilyn Edwards

Hush

In those quiet moments
When all is gleam and dim
I think of all I've been through
And yet to pass me still.
I echo in my heart the words that will fulfill
The hurt, the aches, the long forsakes
And the many, many ills.

In quiet times upon reflection
Even though my heart is filled with tears
A quiet whisper then comes into my ears
It echo love, it echo hope, quietly but still
I try to embrace, I try to take it into my own will.

In quiet meditation when my mind is far but distilled
I remember the lonely times in wilderness hill.
In quiet places when my own voice
In my heart is hushed
When many places look like stormy slopes
Where each river tries to lie tranquil
But bustles in the place it is meant to fill.

It echo love, it echo hope

Even though it's not running to its coast
Because the place where it's meant to go is further still.
The ocean depth, my heart it swept, when my life was not fulfilled
But now I know it's all or no to follow the Saviours' will.

Marilyn Edwards

Refresh

Today I sought the Lord with tears
Heaven opened and he appeared
What's wrong my child I heard him say
Come near, let us pray.

I said Lord, it's a hard road
Trouble comes and trouble goes
Like season that's how we change
Sometimes going around in a maze.

My child, my child come let us reason
What did I say, I am around through every season
I never slumber, nor do I sleep
A constant watch over my sheep
Even my angels I have assigned to fight
Cover and protect you even though they are out of sight.

Your tears I see, your tears I know
Everything you experience was dealt with
Long ago
Where you were redeemed and set free
Wipe away your tears my child
This is your season, walk therein
Do not be buffeted or thrown back into sin.

Satan was defeated long time ago
But obviously he does not want you to know
He'll try his tactics, his schemes and plans
When your tears comes he'll tag along
To see how far you will sink
And then he'll think great he wins.

Fear not, fear not, I am here to wipe away your every tear
To hold you up when you are down
So you do not stumble to the ground
When you go through the fire you will not be burnt
Or through the storm you will not be blown.
That's the promise I give to you
If you trust in me I will bring you through.

My word change not and neither do I
For I am the Word come alive
My word will hold, it will refresh
Even when you are going through a test
Just hold on and you will see
You will win the victory.

My yoke is easy and my burden light
Take it upon you and you will be alright
I end with these lasting words
Your tears will only be for a while for
In the morning you will have a smile.

Love Through the Holy Spirit

Jesus do I really love you
I ask myself this question
It posed a question in my head
Do I even know what love is?
I mulled this in my mind
Cause there is so much in life that is so unkind.

Some say love is care
Been there, always near
Putting yourself behind
When you are helping someone to shine.

Love has no limit in what it will do
Love is happy through and through
It smiles even when others are unkind
It does not envy or wring and wine.

Thank you Holy Spirit you are talking to me
And giving me understanding of love to a large degree
It's true to itself and does not hide
It openly shows itself in the light
It wants to touch, to give, to hold
It wants never to be in control.

It humbly waits it turn
Because it knows from it we must learn
It heals the broken heart
And mend relationships worlds apart.

Marilyn Edwards

Peace

Peace that's what I seek
Looking for it in heaps
But many times I just weep
Because what I look for I don't seem able to keep.

Problems, issues, using lots of tissues
Crying through tough times
Looking, praying but sometimes swaying
Looking for answers that's mine.

People trying your patience
But God gives it as a fruit
How can it blossom without problems?
It's not possible, trials will come
It is how it's dealt with that helps us to overcome.

CHAPTER NINE
REFLECTION

—

Splendor

The cloud it moves across the sky
Like pillars with different shapes as it hides
The heavens deep blue sky, releasing the sun
That shines so bright.

The clouds look thick as it travels along
How God has made it so in his plans
They sometimes look near and sometimes far
Often wondering together or far apart.

If you look up then you will see
The sky go into eternity
Walking along everything moves
The wisdom of God it cannot refuse
For he set them all in their place
Not one is lost or misplaced.

From the clouds the vapor of water comes
Raindrops that travels down.
It loosens its hold at God command
And pours the rain for the earths' charm.

Marilyn Edwards

The heavens declares your handiwork
The clouds as its patterns
The sun through it burst
At night the stars twinkle their light
And the moon is set to make it bright.

How can man say there is no God?
How can he create one with his own hands?
From wood and stone and sometimes gold
The very thing God calls his own.

The clouds from them come mist, rain and hail
It's so beautiful to watch them go pale
And not soon after change to pure white again.

They are set in the sky so blue
But only a few see the beauty that shines through
The sky it speaks, it tells many stories
Just read it and you will understand God's glory.

Love Song

Love with you Lord is so true
I sing it in divine worship to you
A love no other can comprehend
Not a brother, sister or a friend.

It's like sweet scent and fragrance
Enriched in beauty just for you
Its essence cannot be told to another
But you know because you are my Father.

Purity of love you seek
Not just a laughter or a weep
But a love that you can keep.

Love is like new wine
Rich and full bodied all the time
Matured and strengthened each waking day
A love that never goes away.

Love does not hurt, it does not ache
So you know it is not a fake
When the rain does not fall
And the sun does not shine
You know that, that love is still divine.

**Marilyn Edwards

It's warm, bright and shows through dark and dreary light
A love that is matchless and without word
It's a love that only you Lord can give
Because it speaks truth from the heart
Like water it continues to flow
And when it showers you know it has fully grown.

Yokes are broken with this love
So I pray this love will never cease
Unmeasurable, untouchable it will always be.

Reflective

Initiative it drives, makes you come alive
Reflective innocence others make to look so dense
Honesty, purity what's its recompense
No to you it may not make sense.

Reflective, collective memories hidden inside the mind
Waiting to be explained, but may be opposed
It's not your fault so hold your post
For all have voices to call
It may hurt or it may cause one to fall.

Reflective, the heart it boils
Such pain in it is coiled
Sudden hurt, no place to birth
A stump, a punch the thoughts they come
Opinion! Opinion! Yes it comes from some
But they don't understand
They can only see one plan.

Think it, speak it, no more secrets
It's all out in the open
No more hiding behind the curtain
Reflection now it's in hand.

Structured

Yes Lord, I hear your voice
Structure, restoration is my choice
No more if and when it should be
Or waiting impatiently.

Your voice which speaks loud and clear
It whispers so only I can hear
It tells me what to do
But only if I listen I will not be confused.

Help me Lord to hear what you say
No longer going along another way
Prompting and leading is the ultimate place
Lord I therefore seek your face.

Restructure, restore, replace and tear off the disgrace
No you're not poor but rich
If only you can persist in the essence of it
Your toil and labour will declare
That Jesus Christ is there
It never finishes nor does it ache
When he is in the place you take.

Imagine

Imagine a world without people
Imagine
Imagine a sea that stood still
Imagine
Imagine a world without money
Imagine
Imagine there was no hill
Imagine
Imagine the rain did not fall
Imagine
Imagine the sun that did not warm
Imagine
Imagine if some people were not short and some not tall
Imagine
Imagine if we had no friends
Imagine
Imagine all the animals had never been
Imagine
Imagine Jesus Christ did not die and rose again
Imagine
Imagine there was no resurrection
Imagine
How can you imagine these things when it is impossible to imagine.

CHAPTER TEN
MEMORIES

—

My Favourite Person

Grandad was always neatly dressed
Whether at home or going outdoors
His hair was thick with white streaks of grey
But with a nice sheen that matched his brown shiny skin.

He always used to bounce me on his lap
Where if we had not had chairs
I would have been permanently sat.

He would tell me stories about the past
The good times
When he met grandma and their courting
The bad times when he experienced
Racial abuse and exploitation.

He would look sad as he spoke about the hard times they had
When they came to this country
He would say to me, "All people are one
But there are those who think of themselves as being superior
They just take but do not give
Watch out for these people as you grow
And do not become one of them".

He was such a warm person
I felt sorry just at the thought of anyone treating him badly
I never really understood then what he was saying.

My grandad
I used to tell my friends, I had "sweet lap" at home
Always there waiting for me to come home from school
I never did tell them what I meant.

Then one day Grandad became ill
I remember the cold look on his face
The emptiness in his eyes
And through his eyes the loneliness and sorrow in his soul.

Tears filled my eyes to see him suffering
He would say to me, "child why are you crying"
I'm going to be fine, nothing to cry over
But deep down I knew what nature had in store for my grandad.

Finally when it happened
After a long heartbreaking year
I was glad not with the joy of happiness
But joy to see he was no longer suffering.

On his bed the morning it happened
He said to me "Mari, live your life with reason
For we are all Gods' children
No one better and no one worse
So do not ever let any man put you down".

I felt sorry for Grandad. His soul never rested until
The day he died.
Grandad, my sweet granddad.

━ ━

Marilyn Edwards

Marilyn Edwards